CHART PATTERN

PRADEEP KUMAR

I want to dedicate this book to people who want to trade
but not the knowlledge of the chart.

Contents

Preface

There are many chart patterns given in this book and I have written a theory per chart with the help of which trading will be easy. I have made this book only for education purposes. If there is a loss in trading then there will be no responsibility of the author. There was only one purpose of writing this book so that the people who are new to trading can become easy in trading.

Author
pradeep kumar

Foreword

This book explains how to trade in the stock market or any trading platform by looking at the chart and understanding it.This book contains 16+ charts which makes trading easy.Different chart patterns are given in this book and how to trade with each chart is explained.

Acknowledgements

"I want to thank those people because of whom I learned trading. Some big traders taught with the help of YouTube and in live classes."

Prologue

About This Book ?
    what is chart patterns.
    types of chart patterns.
    Best Chart Patterns.
    1.Head and shoulders
2.Double top
3.Double bottom
4.Rounding bottom
5.Cup and handle
6.Wedges
7.Pennant or flags
8.Ascending triangle
9.Descending triangle
10.Symmetrical triangle

ONE

ABOUT THIS BOOK

The book explains about trading "Chart Patterns".In which 10 types of chart patterns are given with complete details.With the help of this book, you will be able to do trading easily because you can also keep this book in your pocket.

This book is explained in the easiest way, with the help of which trading is very easy. With the help of this book, you can easily create patterns while trading.

TWO

WHAT IS "CHART PATTERNS"

Patterns are the distinctive formations created by the movements of security prices on a chart. A pattern is identified by a line that connects common price points, such as closing prices or highs or lows, during a specific period of time.

10 chart patterns every trader needs to know

Chart patterns are an integral aspect of technical analysis, but they require some getting used to before they can be used effectively. To help you get to grips with them, here are 10 chart patterns every trader needs to know.

THREE

Types Of Chart Patterns

Chart patterns fall broadly into three categories:

1. continuation patterns,
2. reversal patterns
3. bilateral patterns.

Best chart patterns

1.Head and shoulders
2.Double top
3.Double bottom
4.Rounding bottom
5.Cup and handle
6.Wedges
7.Pennant or flags
8.Ascending triangle
9.Descending triangle
10.Symmetrical triangle

FOUR

HEAD & SHOULDER

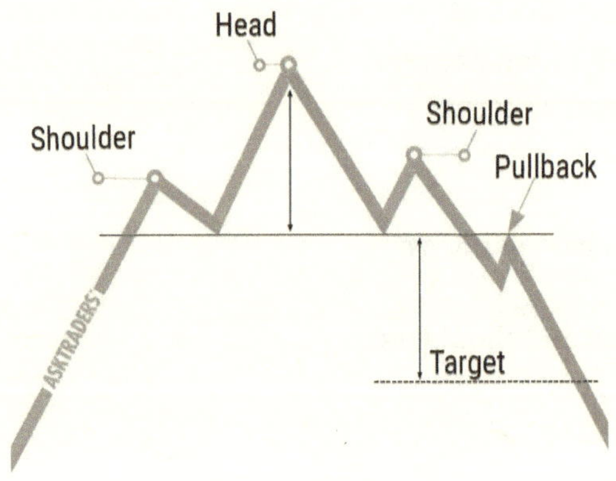

H & S Pattern

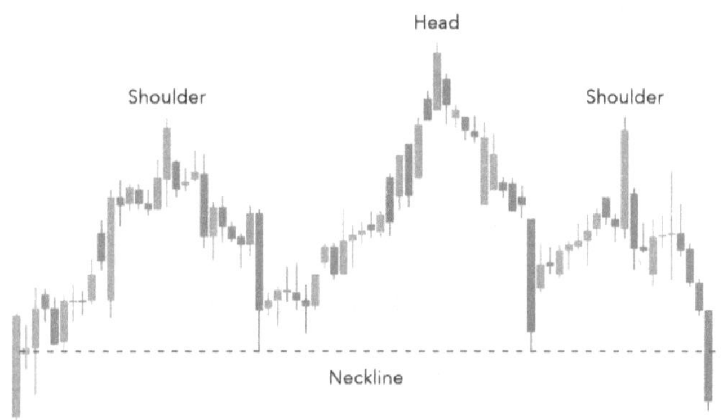

Head & shoulder

The Head and Shoulders chart pattern is a price reversal pattern that helps traders identify when a reversal may be underway after a trend has exhausted itself. This reversal signals the end of an uptrend. The Head and Shoulders pattern has a distinctive appearance resembling its namesake which includes a distinct 'left shoulder', 'head', 'right shoulder' and 'neckline' formation.

FIVE

INVERSE H&S PATTERNS

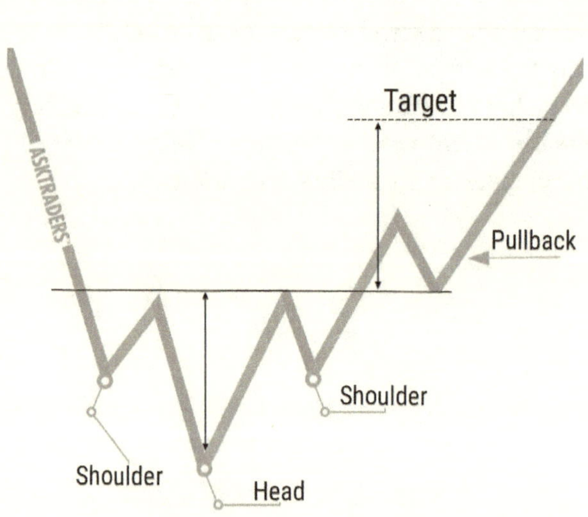

inverse H&S

I

The Inverse Head and Shoulders (informally known as the 'Reverse Head and Shoulders pattern) resembles the same structure as the standard foration but reversed. The Inverse Head and Shoulders is observable in a downtrend (see image below) and indicates a reversal of a downtrend as higher lows are created.

SIX

DOUBLE TOP

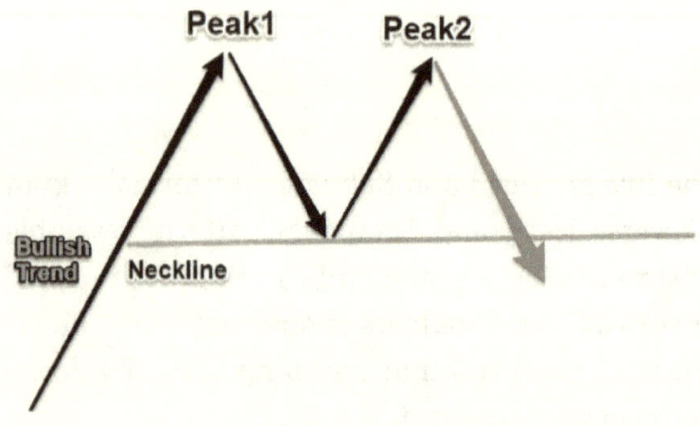

DOUBLE TOP

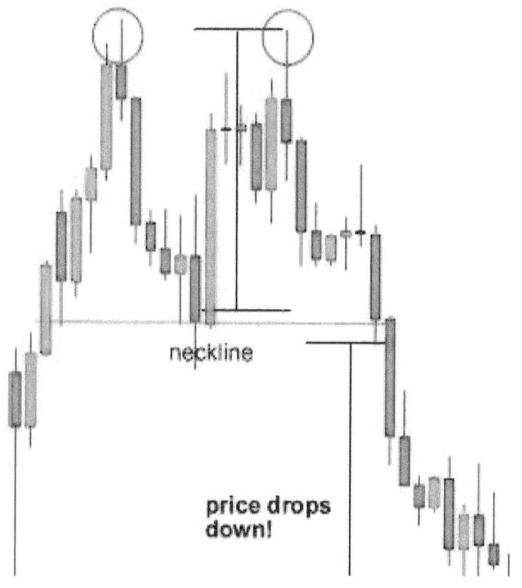

DOUBLE TOP

A double top is another pattern that traders use to highlight trend reversals. Typically, an asset's price will experience a peak, before retracing back to a level of support. It will then climb up once more before reversing back more permanently against the prevailing trend.

SEVEN

DOUBLE BOTTOM

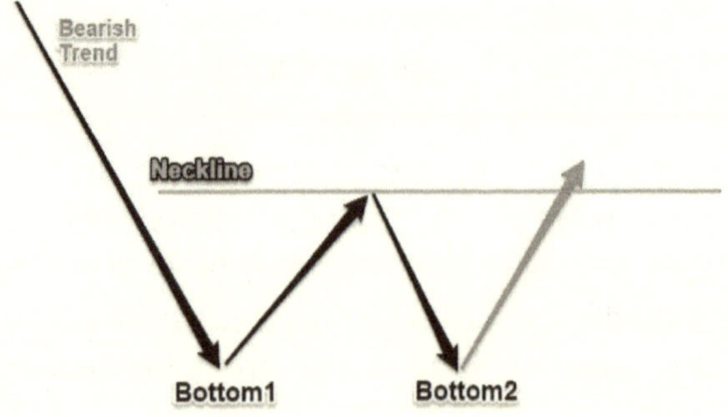

DOUBLE BOTTOM

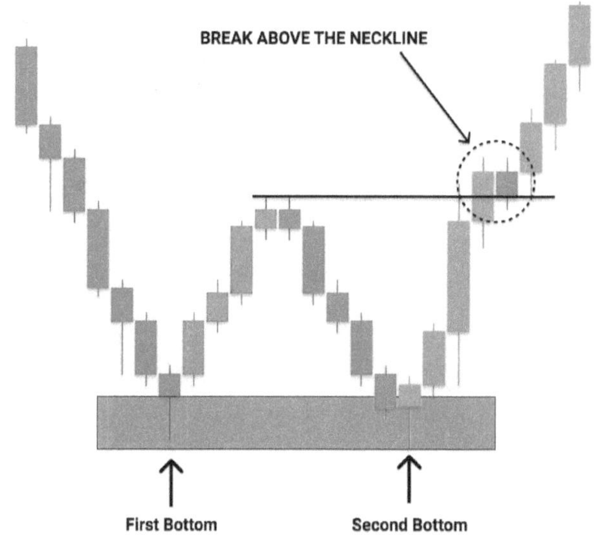

Double bottom

A double bottom chart pattern indicates a period of selling, causing an asset's price to drop below a level of support. It will then rise to a level of resistance, before dropping again. Finally, the trend will reverse and begin an upward motion as the market becomes more bullish.

EIGHT

RISING WADGE

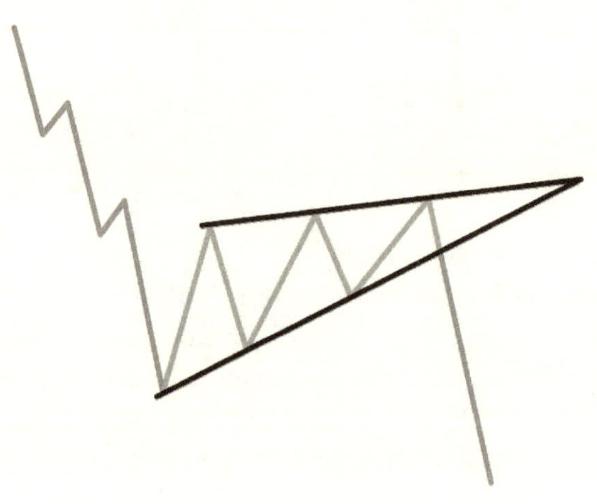

RISING WADGE

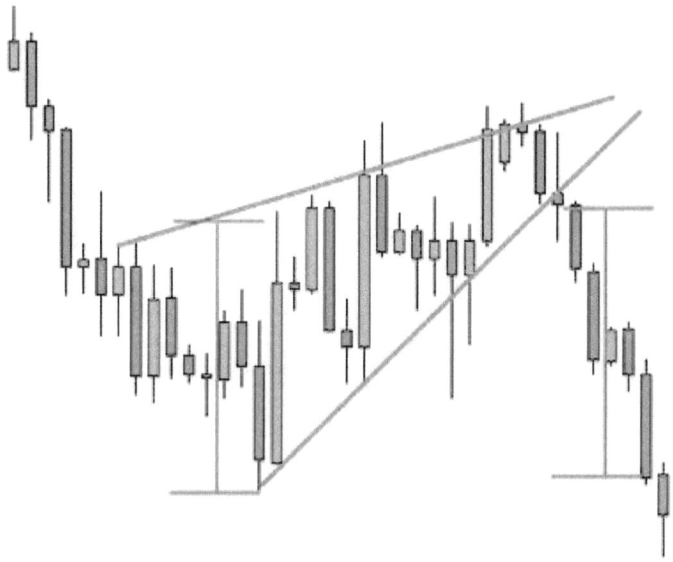

RISING WADGE

A rising wedge is represented by a trend line caught between two upwardly slanted lines of support and resistance. In this case the line of support is steeper than the resistance line. This pattern generally signals that an asset's price will eventually decline more permanently – which is demonstrated when it breaks through the support level.

NINE
FALLING WADGE

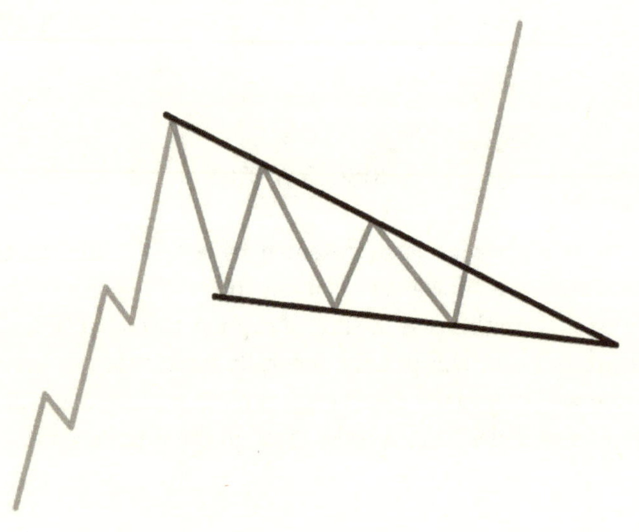

FALLING WADGE

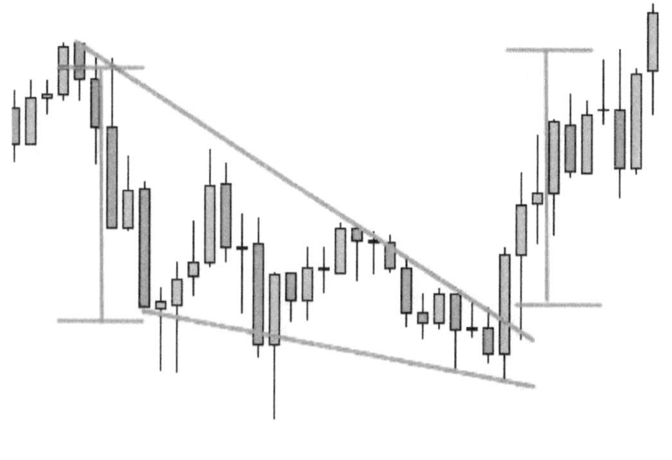

F-W

A falling wedge occurs between two downwardly sloping levels. In this case the line of resistance is steeper than the support. A falling wedge is usually indicative that an asset's price will rise and break through the level of resistance, as shown in the example below.

TEN

BULLISH & BEARISH PENNANTS

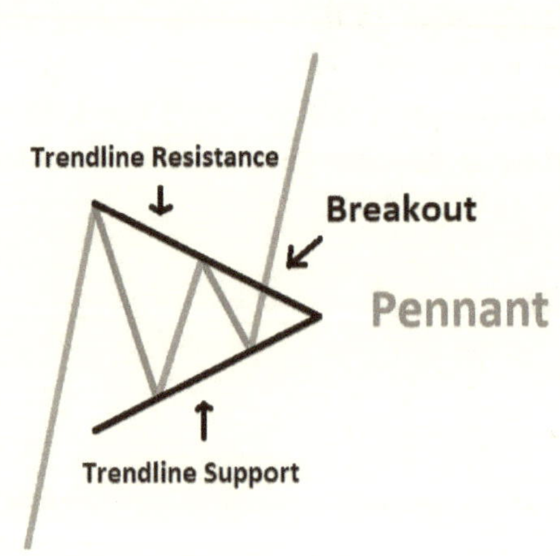

BULLISH PENNANTS

A Bullish Pennants are continuation candlestick patterns that occur in strong uptrends. The Pennant is formed from an upward flagpole, a consolidation period and then the continuation of the uptrend after a breakout. Traders look for a break above the Pennant to take advantage of the renewed bullishmomentum.

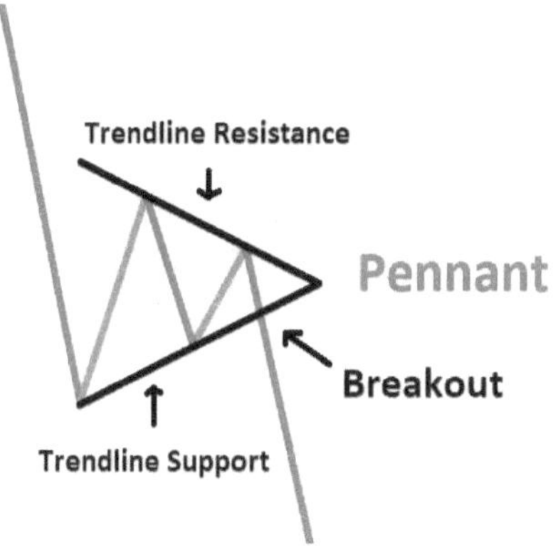

BEARISH PENNENTS

Bearish Pennants are simply the opposite of the Bullish Pennant. Bearish Pennants are continuation patterns that occur in strong downtrends. They always start with a flagpole – a steep drop in price, followed by a pause in the downward movement.

ELEVEN

BULLISH RECTANGLE

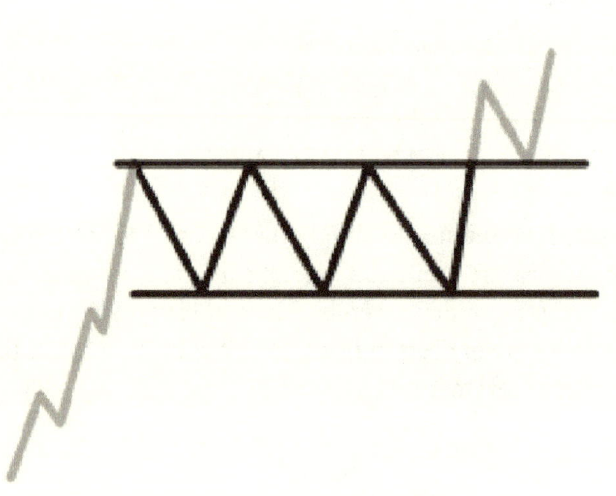

BULLISH RECTANGLE

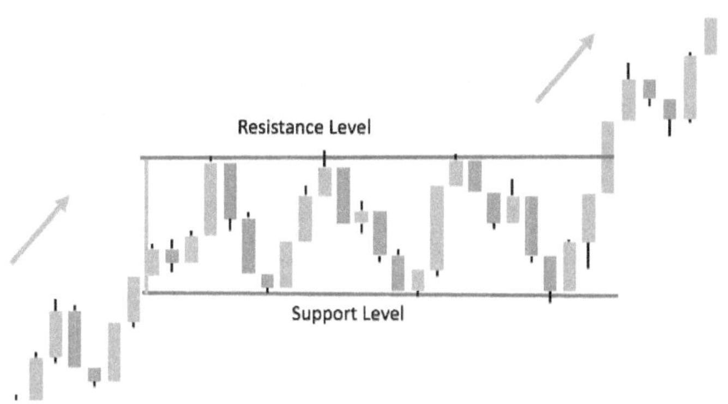

B-RECT...

Bearish Pennants are simply the opposite of the Bullish Pennant. Bearish Pennants are continuation patterns that occur in strong downtrends. They always start with a flagpole – a steep drop in price, followed by a pause in the downward movement.

TWELVE

BEARISH RECTANGLE

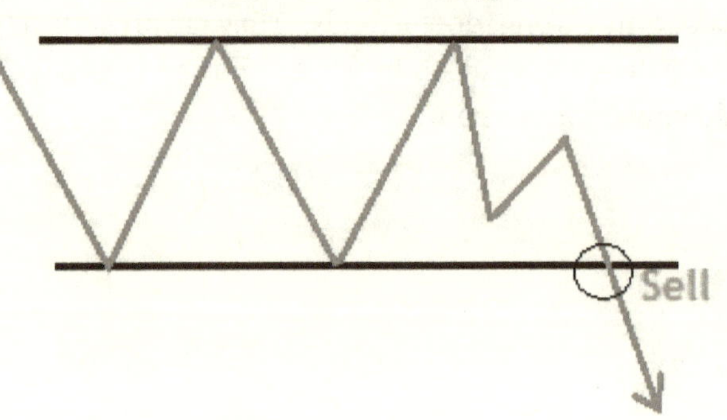

B--R

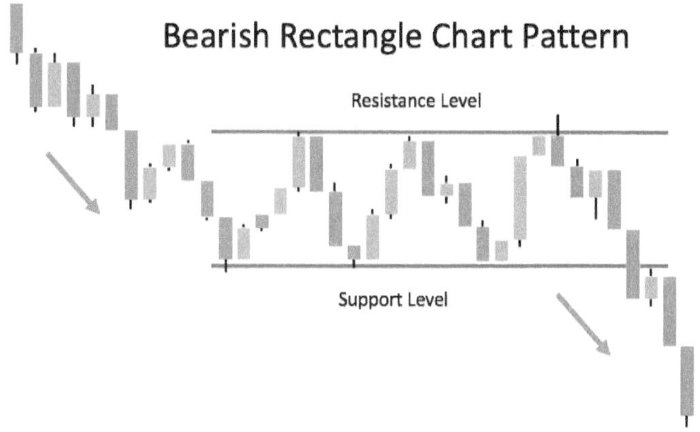

B--R

A continuation pattern occurring in a downtrend, whereby traders look to enter into short positions once price breaks support and closes inside the 'breakout zone'.

THIRTEEN

BEAR & BULL FLAG

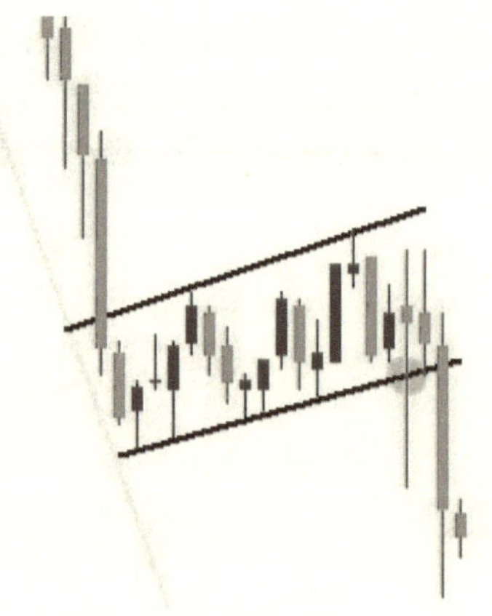

BEAR FLAG

The Bear flag pattern develops in a bearish trend or when a bearish trend is about to be formed and when sellers/bears are in control.

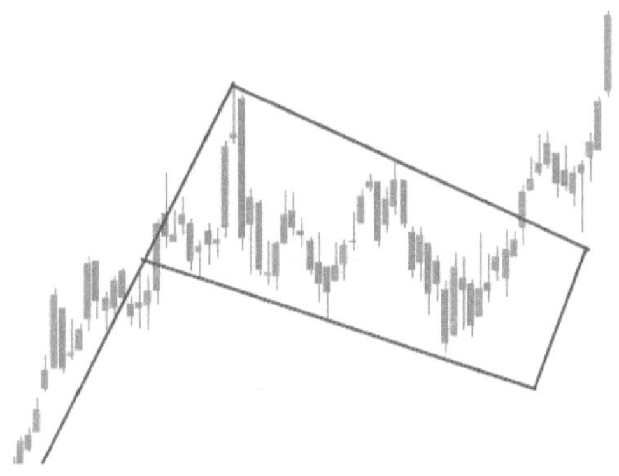

BULL FLAG

The bull flag pattern forms mostly in a bullish trend or when a bullish trend is about to be formed and when buyers/bulls are in control of the market.

FOURTEEN

SYMMETRICAL TRAINGLE

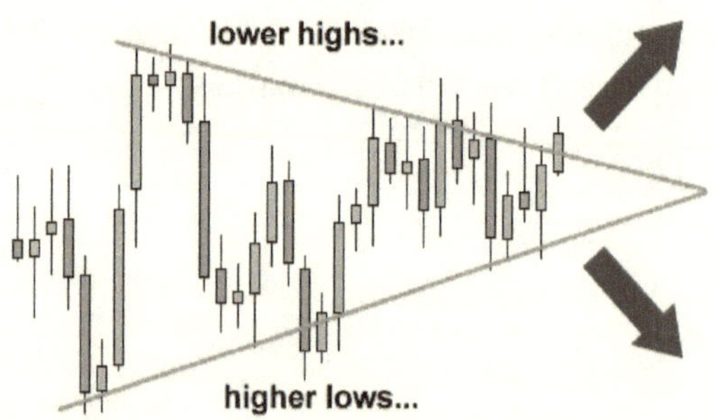

symmetrical T.

The symmetrical triangle pattern can be either bullish or bearish, depending on the market. In either case, it is normally a continuation pattern, which means the market will usually continue in the same direction as the overall trend once the pattern has formed.

FIFTEEN

DESCENDING TRAINGLE

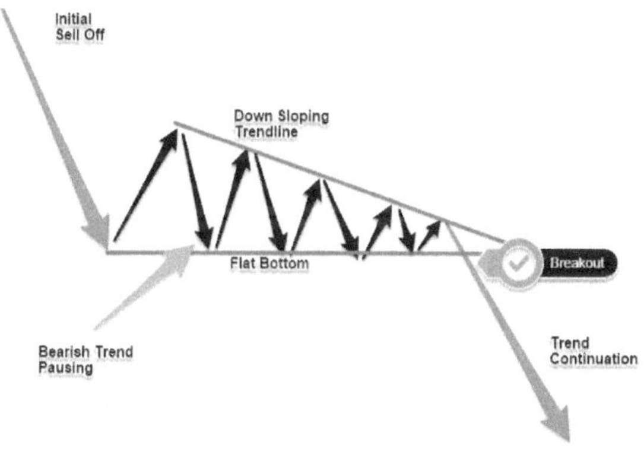

descending

Descending triangles generally shift lower and break through the support because they are indicative of a market dominated by sellers, meaning that successively lower peaks are likely to be prevalent and unlikely to reverse.

SIXTEEN

ASCENDING TRAINGLE

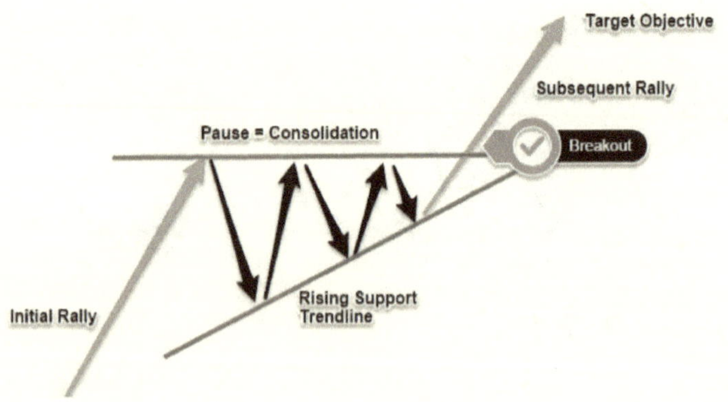

ascending

The ascending triangle is a bullish continuation pattern which signifies the continuation of an uptrend. Ascending triangles can be drawn onto charts by placing a horizontal line along the swing highs – the resistance & then drawing an ascending trend line along the swing lows – the support.